SAINT FAUSTINA

DIARY

Join young Helena Kowalska on a heart-warming adventure as she becomes Saint Faustina, the "Apostle of Divine Mercy." In this beautifully illustrated 71-page book, watch as Jesus' gentle voice leads her to paint the world with mercy, record His loving messages in her diary and light a spark of trust in every heart

Inside you'll discover:
- A captivating story of vision and service, told in simple text for young readers and deeper reflections for older readers
- Coloring scenes that bring Faustina's garden, chapel, and the Divine Mercy image to life
- Engaging puzzles and a maze that guide young readers back to the chapel of mercy
- "Divine Mercy Chaplet card" to help children pray and reflect on kindness, forgiveness and trusting God

Perfect for bedtime reading, family devotions, or Sunday School, Little Hearts of Mercy is an interactive journey into God's unfailing love—one that will inspire children to see and share mercy every day

Attributions:
"Used with permission of the Marian Fathers of the Immaculate Conception of the B.V.M."
"The Congregation of the Sisters of Our Lady of Mercy"
https://www.saint-faustina.org/biography/

Written, Designed and Published in the USA

DEDICATION

To our beloved brother Dipin,
whose quiet, fervent devotion to the Divine Mercy became
the first lamp along our pilgrimage towards Divine Mercy.
Your prayers have been our refuge,
your counsel our compass,
and your steadfast encouragement the gentle current that
carried this work to shore.
May Christ—Mercy Incarnate—
enfold you in the brilliance of His Sacred Heart,
grant you the graces you so abundantly impart to others,
and lead your every step as you continue to lead others
toward the wellspring of His inexhaustible love

Love Diya & Joby

Sister Faustina entered the world on a bright summer morning, August 25, 1905, in the peaceful Polish village of Głogowiec. She was the third of ten children born to Marianna Babel and Stanisław Kowalski, who had settled on a small farm they purchased just after their wedding. There, nestled far from dusty roads and bustling towns, they built a cozy, single-story cottage and sturdy barns—creating a warm home where little Helena Kowalska (later Sister Faustina) would grow up surrounded by love, hard work and quiet fields

4

Every Kowalski child was carried to the tiny parish church of St. Casimir in Świnice Warckie to be welcomed into God's family. On 27 August 1905, Father Józef Chodyński recorded the baptism of Helena, born in Głogowiec on 25 August to Stanisław and Marianna Babel. Her godparents were Konstanty Bednarek and Marianna Szewczyk (Szczepaniak)

The Kowalski home moved to a gentle rhythm: prayer first, work second. Father greeted dawn with hymns, reminding even sleepy children that God must come first. Holy images and a tiny altar dominated the bedroom, and each night the family knelt together. Month of May brought the Loreto Litany at the garden chapel; October, the rosary; Sunday afternoons, Father's readings from Lives of the Saints

Yet little Helenka was different from the other village children. Her mother often found her slipping out of bed at night to kneel and pray. Worried, she scolded gently, "You'll wear yourself out, child!"
Helenka only smiled. "But, Mama," she whispered, "an angel taps me awake to pray"

"When I was seven, [it happened] during Vespers and Jesus was exposed in the monstrance. The Lord granted me understanding of the things of God" (Diary 1404)

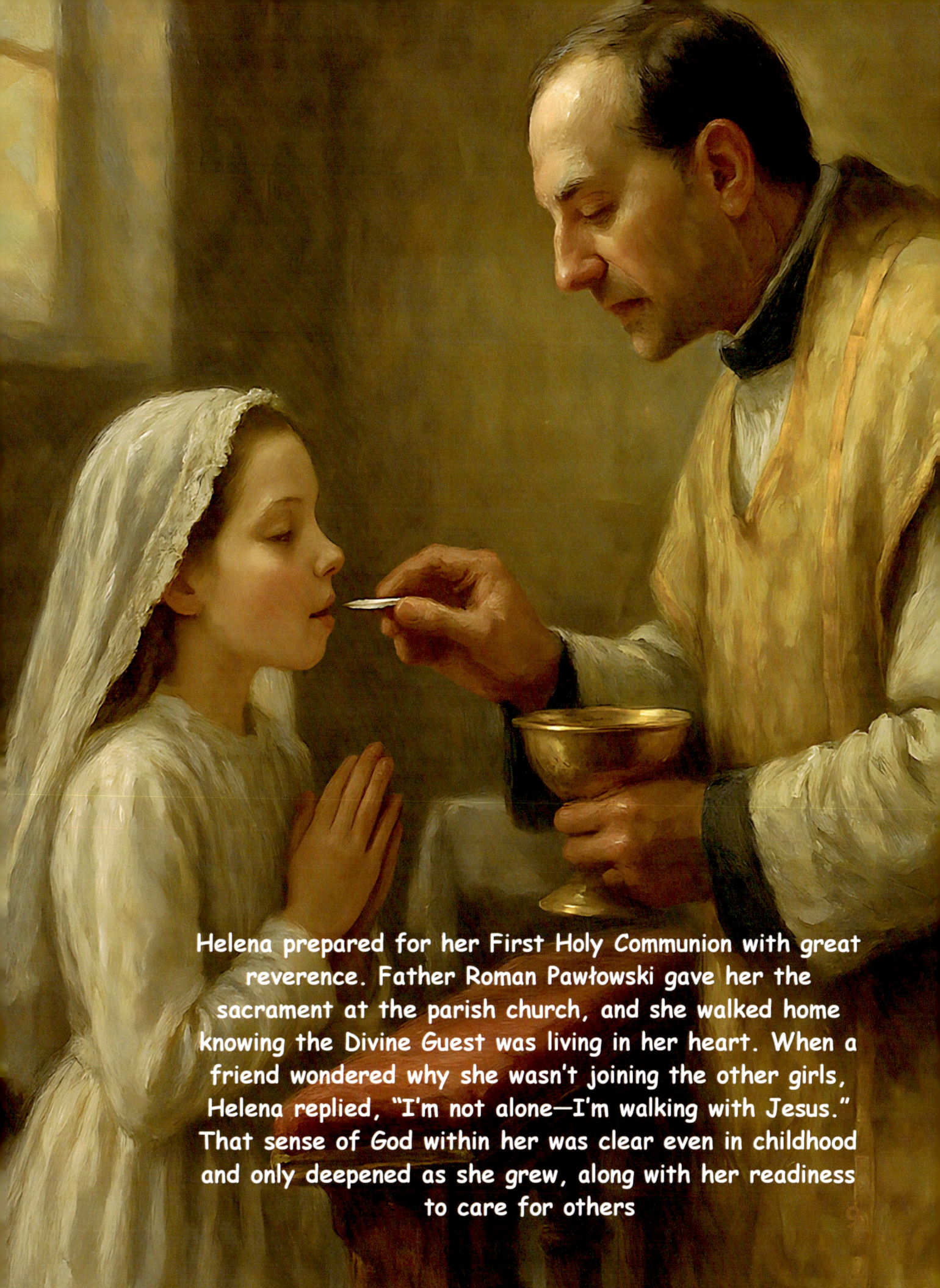

Helena prepared for her First Holy Communion with great reverence. Father Roman Pawłowski gave her the sacrament at the parish church, and she walked home knowing the Divine Guest was living in her heart. When a friend wondered why she wasn't joining the other girls, Helena replied, "I'm not alone—I'm walking with Jesus." That sense of God within her was clear even in childhood and only deepened as she grew, along with her readiness to care for others

Even as a little girl, she was known for her kind heart. She noticed anyone who was hungry or in need and always looked for ways to help—whether that meant giving bread, sharing what she had, or finding other ways to care for them

Once, she dressed in her mother's worn clothes, pretended to be a beggar, and visited every house in the village. The coins she received she carried straight to the parish priest for the poor. "Everyone adored her," her mother remembered. 'She was the most thoughtful of my children—modest and quiet, quick to help with any chore, yet always cheerful and smiling"

Even as a child, her brother Stanisław remembered, "she loved to tell us about saints, wandering pilgrims, and hermits who lived on roots, berries, and wild honey. To delight our father, she would pull Lives of the Saints or another holy book from our tiny bookcase and read it aloud. She learned the stories by heart, and the next day—while we tended the cattle—she could recite every word to us and to anyone nearby. She often said that one day she would join a convent. We only laughed; we simply couldn't understand her"

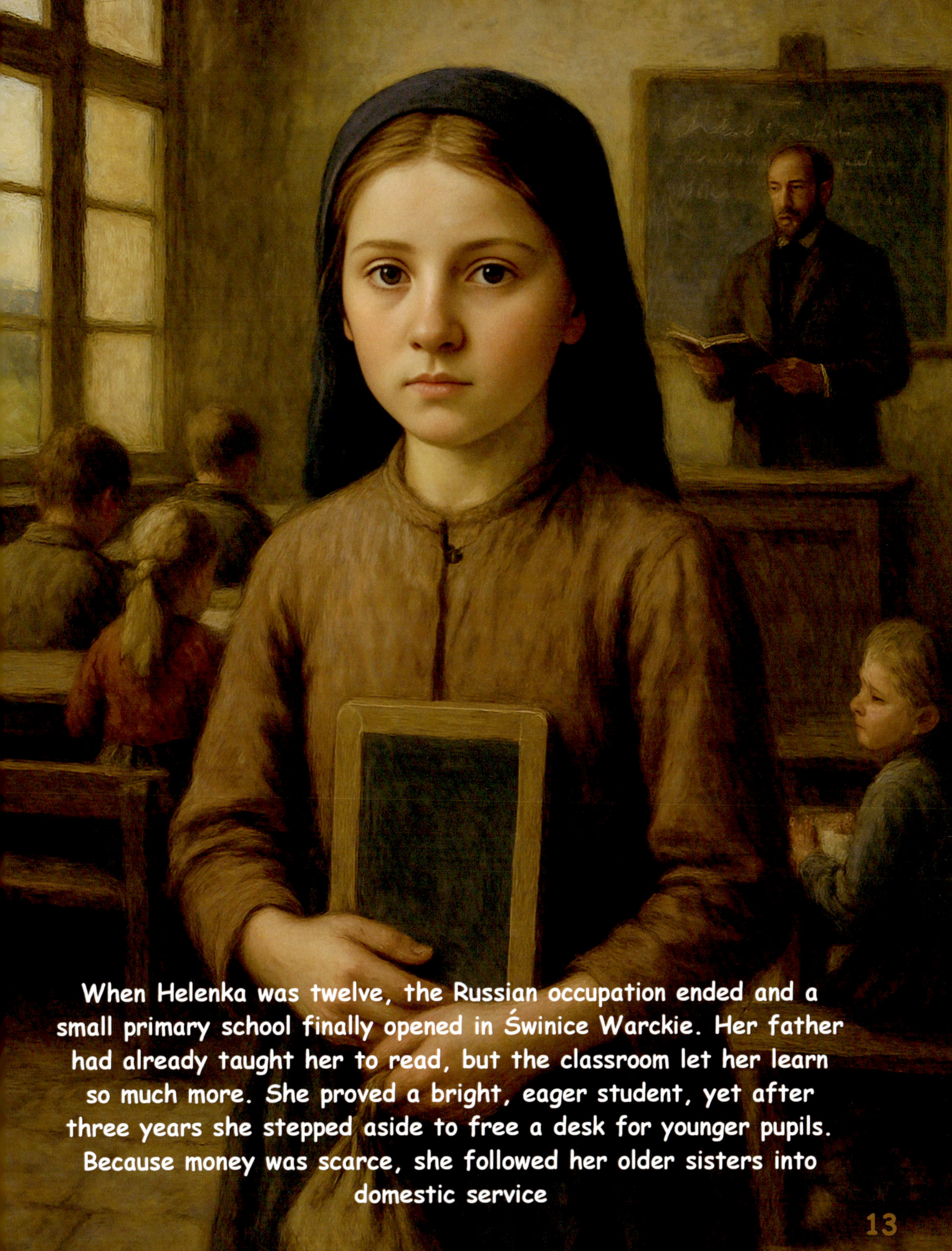

When Helenka was twelve, the Russian occupation ended and a small primary school finally opened in Świnice Warckie. Her father had already taught her to read, but the classroom let her learn so much more. She proved a bright, eager student, yet after three years she stepped aside to free a desk for younger pupils. Because money was scarce, she followed her older sisters into domestic service

13

At sixteen Helenka left home for Aleksandrów Łódzki to work in the Bryszewski family's bakery-shop. She cooked, cleaned, fetched water, delivered meals to the staff, and minded their little boy, Zenek. "She did nearly everything," Zenek later said, "yet still found time to play with me"

14

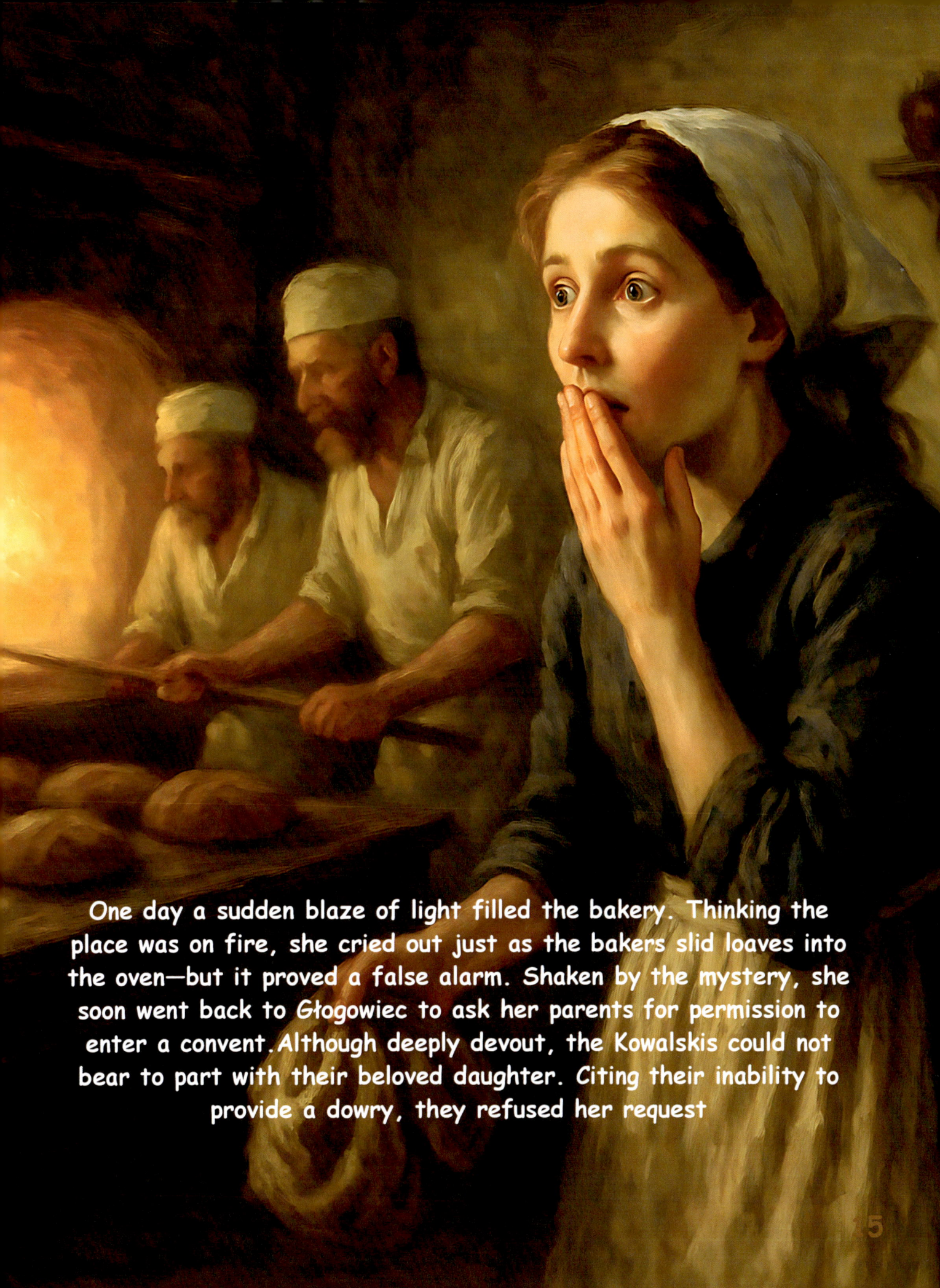

One day a sudden blaze of light filled the bakery. Thinking the place was on fire, she cried out just as the bakers slid loaves into the oven—but it proved a false alarm. Shaken by the mystery, she soon went back to Głogowiec to ask her parents for permission to enter a convent. Although deeply devout, the Kowalskis could not bear to part with their beloved daughter. Citing their inability to provide a dowry, they refused her request

5

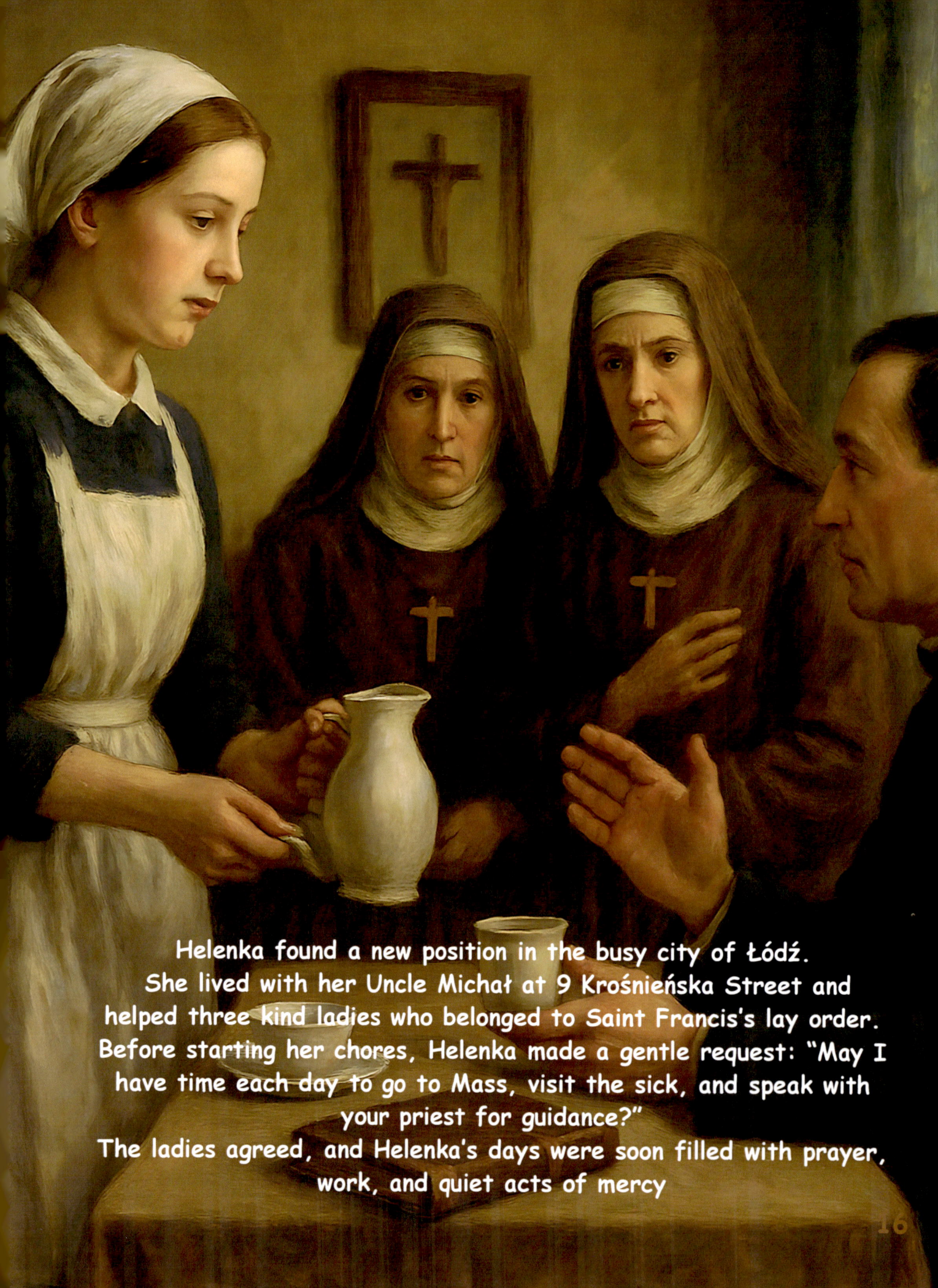

Helenka found a new position in the busy city of Łódź.
She lived with her Uncle Michał at 9 Krośnieńska Street and
helped three kind ladies who belonged to Saint Francis's lay order.
Before starting her chores, Helenka made a gentle request: "May I
have time each day to go to Mass, visit the sick, and speak with
your priest for guidance?"
The ladies agreed, and Helenka's days were soon filled with prayer,
work, and quiet acts of mercy

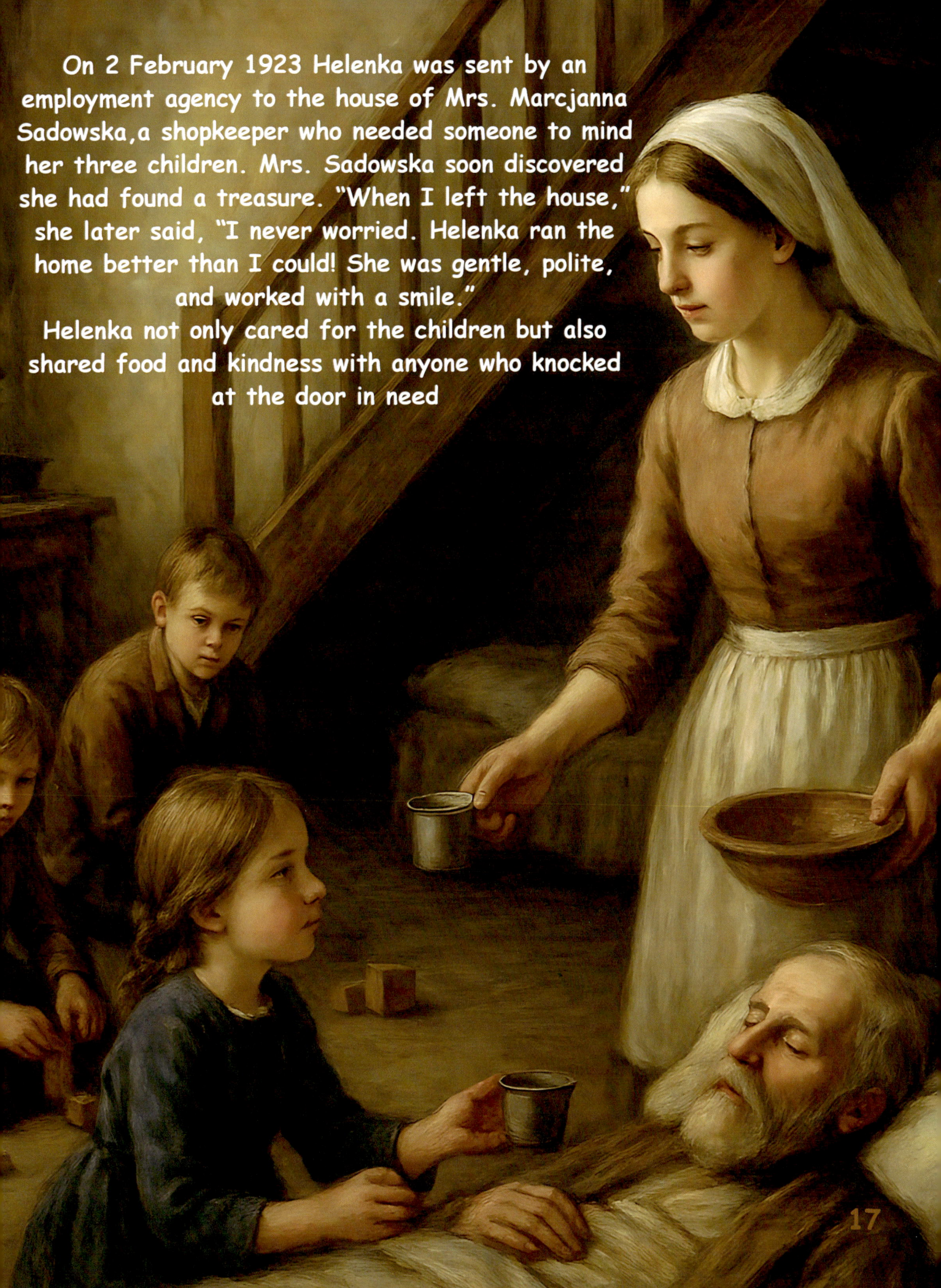

On 2 February 1923 Helenka was sent by an employment agency to the house of Mrs. Marcjanna Sadowska, a shopkeeper who needed someone to mind her three children. Mrs. Sadowska soon discovered she had found a treasure. "When I left the house," she later said, "I never worried. Helenka ran the home better than I could! She was gentle, polite, and worked with a smile."
Helenka not only cared for the children but also shared food and kindness with anyone who knocked at the door in need

17

When Helenka turned eighteen, she again begged her parents to let her join a convent, but they still said no. "After that refusal I indulged in the vanity of life, not paying any attention to the voice of grace, although there was nothing in which my soul could find contentment. The continual calling of grace was a great torment for me, nonetheless I tried to stifle my calling with various entertainments" (Diary 8)

One evening she went to a dance in Wenecja Park. The music had only just begun when she suddenly saw Jesus standing beside her, bruised and covered with wounds. 'How long am I to put up with you, and how long are you going to keep Me waiting'?" (Diary 9). Helenka's heart ached. At that moment she knew she could no longer push His call aside

Pretending she had a headache, Helenka slipped away from the dance and hurried to the nearest church—the great Cathedral of St. Stanisław Kostka. She knelt before the Blessed Sacrament and pleaded, "Lord, show me what to do!" In the stillness of her prayer she heard the answer: "Go immediately to Warsaw, there you will enter a convent" (Diary 10)

Helenka didn't hesitate. Without waiting for her parents' permission, she packed her small bundle and set off for the capital, determined to follow God's call

19

Needing guidance, Helenka went to the pastor of St. James Parish, Father Jakub Dąbrowski, who wrote a short note and sent her to Ostrówek, to the home of Mr. and Mrs. Samuel and Aldona Lipszyc. The Lipszyc household became a safe harbor. Helenka cared for the children, sang as she worked, and quietly saved her wages for a simple convent dowry. "I will always remember her bright, wholesome smile," Mrs. Lipszyc recalled years later. "She sang all the time, especially the hymn she taught me:
'I am to revere Jesus hidden in the Sacrament'

The Lipszyc family treated Helenka like their own daughter. Everyone admired her cheerful spirit and the gentle way she cared for the children. Mrs. Lipszyc even tried to match her with a husband, certain Helenka would make a wonderful wife and mother. But Helenka's heart longed for something more

"It happened one day during the octave of Corpus Christi – she recorded the most important event of her time at Ostrówek in her diary – God filled my soul with an inner light enabling me to come to know Him as the Supreme Good and Beauty. I learned how much God loved me. Eternal is His love for me. It was during Vespers – in simple words straight from my heart I made a vow of perpetual chastity to God. From that moment on I felt a greater intimacy with God, my Bridegroom. Since that moment I have had a little cell in my heart, in which I have always dwelled with Jesus" (Diary16)

Helenka rode the train from Ostrówek into Warsaw, calling at
convent after convent, but every gate stayed closed. At last
she came to the Sisters of Our Lady of Mercy. When Mother
Małgorzata spoke with her, she later told Mother General,
"The girl is ordinary—small, thin, a maid by trade, with no
dowry and not even a tiny trousseau. There is nothing
remarkable about her." Mother Leonarda, hearing this,
doubted whether someone so poor and unassuming would ever
fit into their community

At last, on 1 August 1925—the vigil of Our Lady, Queen of Angels—Helenka Kowalska stepped across the convent threshold. "I felt extremely happy, I thought I had entered life in paradise. One big prayer of thanksgiving sprang up from my heart" (Diary 17). Within three weeks, however, she realized the sisters had very little time for private prayer and began thinking of joining a stricter community. One night, lying facedown in prayer, she saw Jesus' wounded face.

"Who has hurt You so much, Jesus?" Jesus replied, "You will cause Me such pain if your leave this Order. Here I have called you, and to no other place; here I have prepared many graces for you" (Diary 19). Ashamed, Helenka withdrew her request at once and resolved to remain where God had placed her

My Mercy does not want that, but justice commands it

Only a few weeks after entering, Mother Superior sent Helenka and two other postulants to Skolimów, a convent in the suburbs.At Skolimów she asked Jesus whom she should pray for. In reply she had a vision of purgatory, from which she learned that the greatest torment of the souls in this misty place, full of fire was longing for God. In her heart of hearts she heard the words, "My Mercy does not want that, but justice commands it" (Diary 20). From that day, Helenka prayed even more earnestly for the souls in purgatory, and God allowed her to feel a special closeness to them

Sister Janina Olga Bartkiewicz, the postulant mistress, combined great kindness with firm expectations. She often said Helenka carried a private, glowing prayer life and must be very dear to Jesus.One of Helenka's classmates, Sister Szymona Nalewajk, marveled at her gentle spirit. "She accepted every little humiliation without a single complaint," Sister Szymona later wrote. "I couldn't believe someone so new could show such patience and goodness." Helenka's quiet strength flowed from her deep desire to imitate Jesus—trusting the Father even in pain, remaining meek and humble, and loving everyone with patient, self-giving care

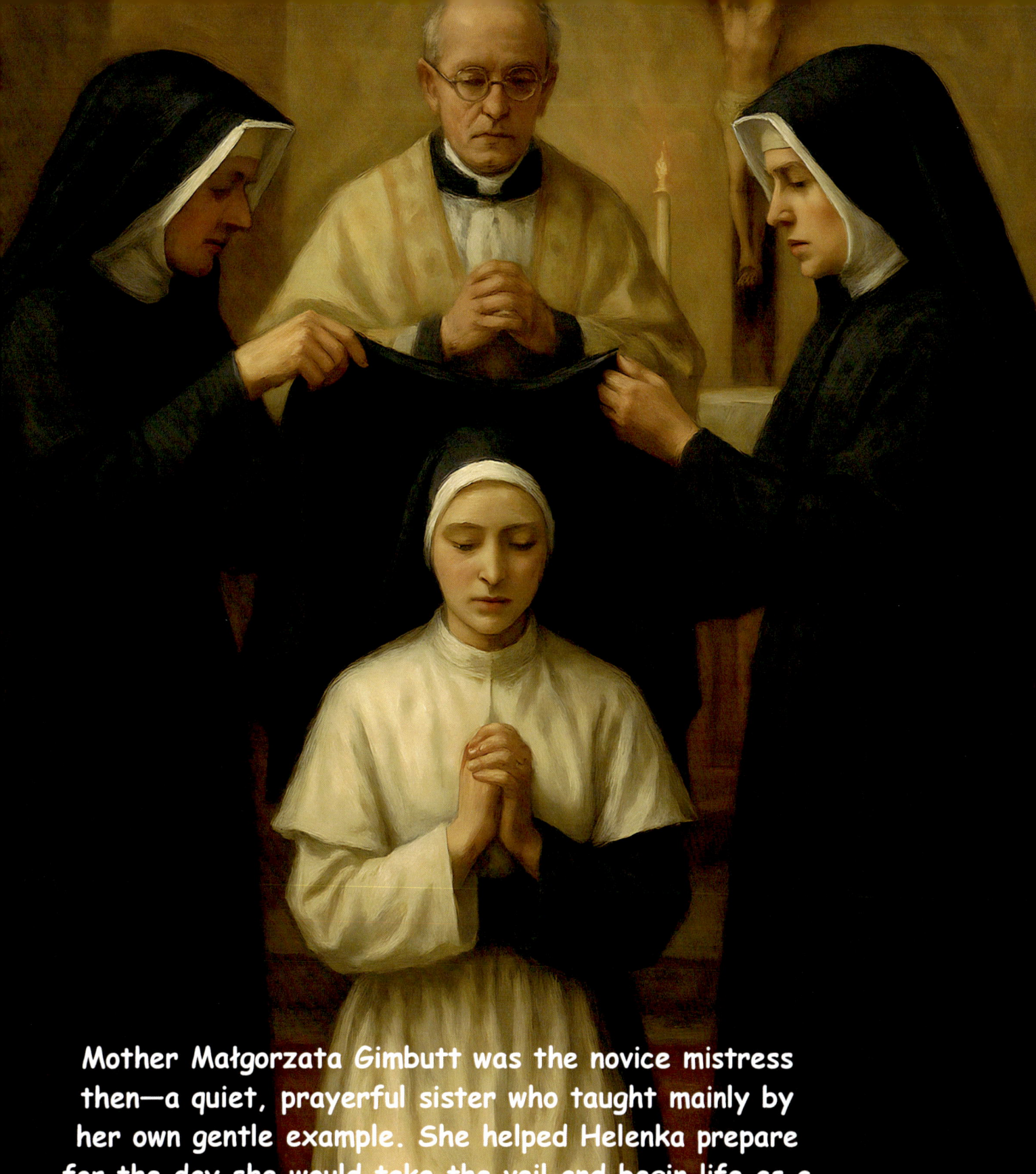

Mother Małgorzata Gimbutt was the novice mistress then—a quiet, prayerful sister who taught mainly by her own gentle example. She helped Helenka prepare for the day she would take the veil and begin life as a novice. On 30 April 1926, during the veil-taking ceremony, Helenka heard the words,
"From now on you will no longer be called by your baptismal name. You shall be Sister Maria Faustina"

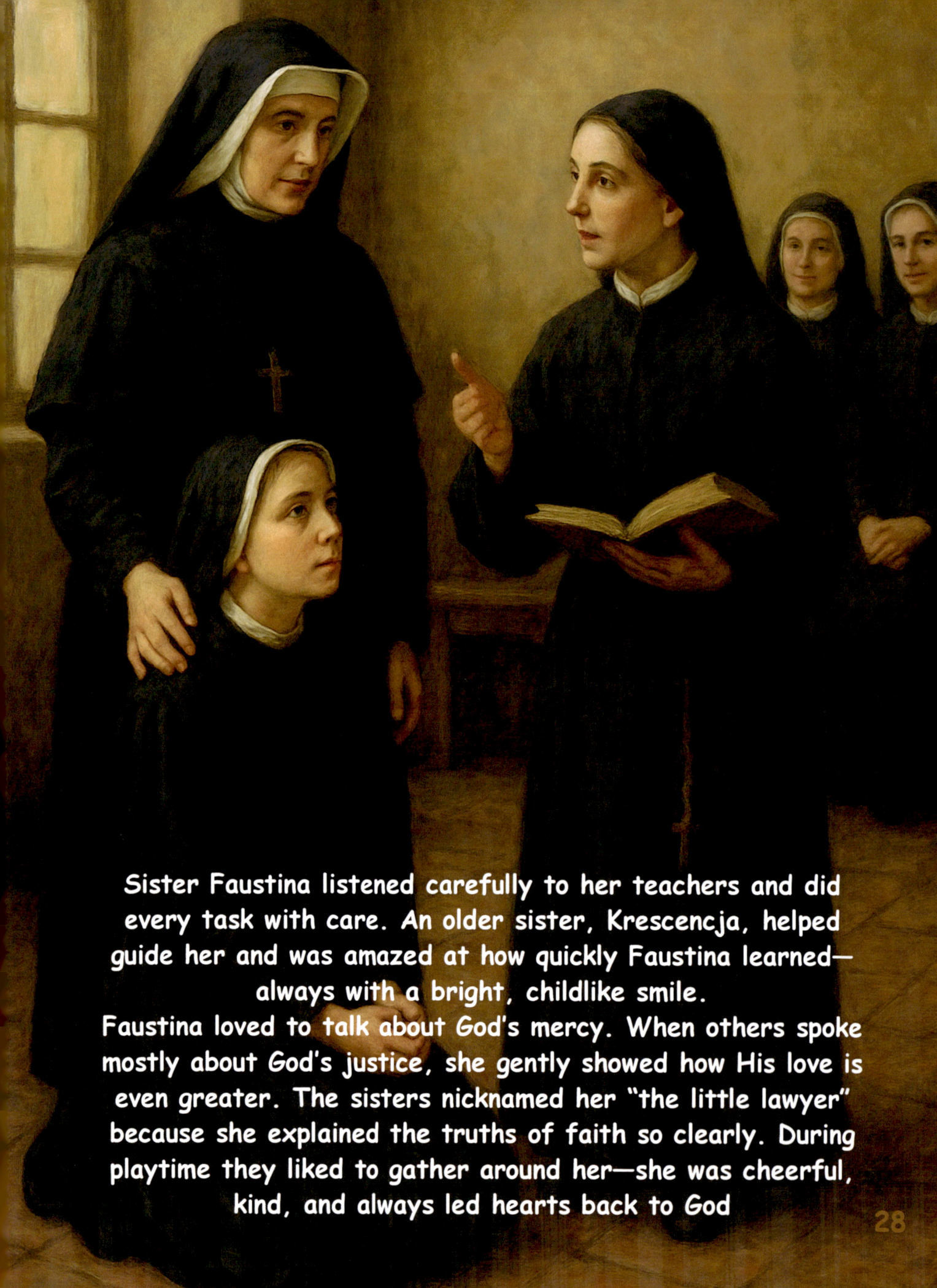

Sister Faustina listened carefully to her teachers and did every task with care. An older sister, Krescencja, helped guide her and was amazed at how quickly Faustina learned—always with a bright, childlike smile.

Faustina loved to talk about God's mercy. When others spoke mostly about God's justice, she gently showed how His love is even greater. The sisters nicknamed her "the little lawyer" because she explained the truths of faith so clearly. During playtime they liked to gather around her—she was cheerful, kind, and always led hearts back to God

Near the end of her first year as a novice, Faustina's bright joy dimmed. Prayers felt heavy, and she found no comfort. For many months she felt very small before God and worried He was far away. Her novice mistress encouraged her, but the struggle grew as the day for vows drew near. Reading was hard, and even in church she felt unsure. Still, her confessor asked her to receive Holy Communion, and Faustina obeyed. At one point, I got a strong feeling that I had been rejected by God. That terrible thought pierced my soul right through. My soul started to die from the suffering. I wanted to die but could not" (Diary 23)

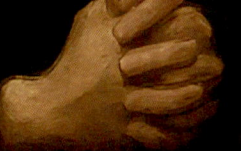

Even on her hardest days, God sent little moments of light and joy. She felt His love again—and Our Lady came close to comfort and help her

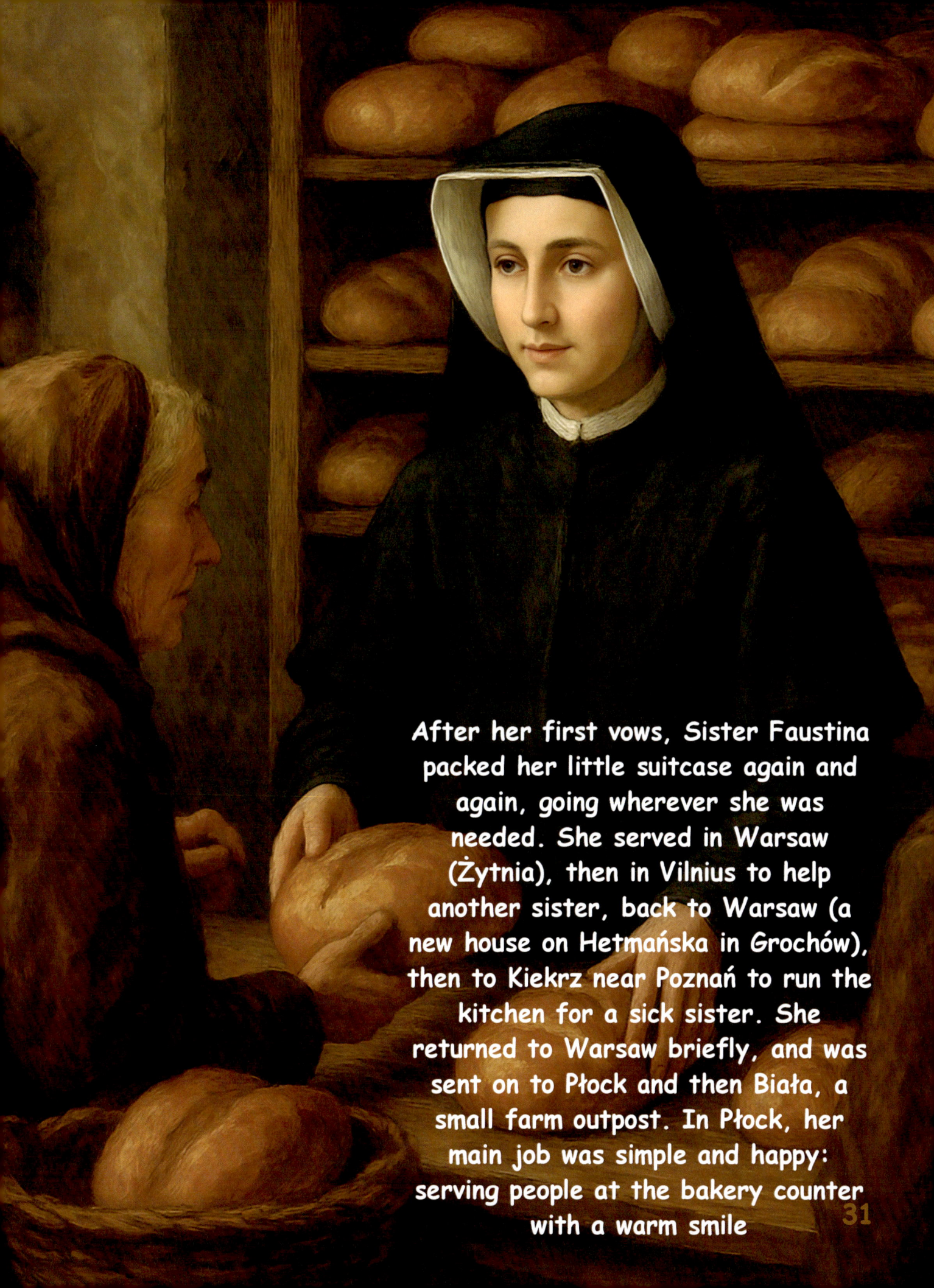

After her first vows, Sister Faustina packed her little suitcase again and again, going wherever she was needed. She served in Warsaw (Żytnia), then in Vilnius to help another sister, back to Warsaw (a new house on Hetmańska in Grochów), then to Kiekrz near Poznań to run the kitchen for a sick sister. She returned to Warsaw briefly, and was sent on to Płock and then Biała, a small farm outpost. In Płock, her main job was simple and happy: serving people at the bakery counter with a warm smile

31

In the convent at Płock, Sister Faustina's special mission began. One Sunday evening (February 22, 1931), In the evening when she returned to her cell, she had a physical vision of Jesus in a white robe. His right hand was lifted up in a gesture of blessing, and His left hand was touching His breast from which two rays, a red one and a pale one, radiated out. After a while Jesus said to her, "Make Me a picture of this image in the form that you see, with the inscription Jesus, I trust in You. I want this picture venerated first in your chapel, and in the whole world. I promise that the soul that venerates this picture shall not perish. I also promise it victory over its enemies, already here on Earth, and especially in the hour of death. I Myself shall protect it as My glory" (Diary 47-48)

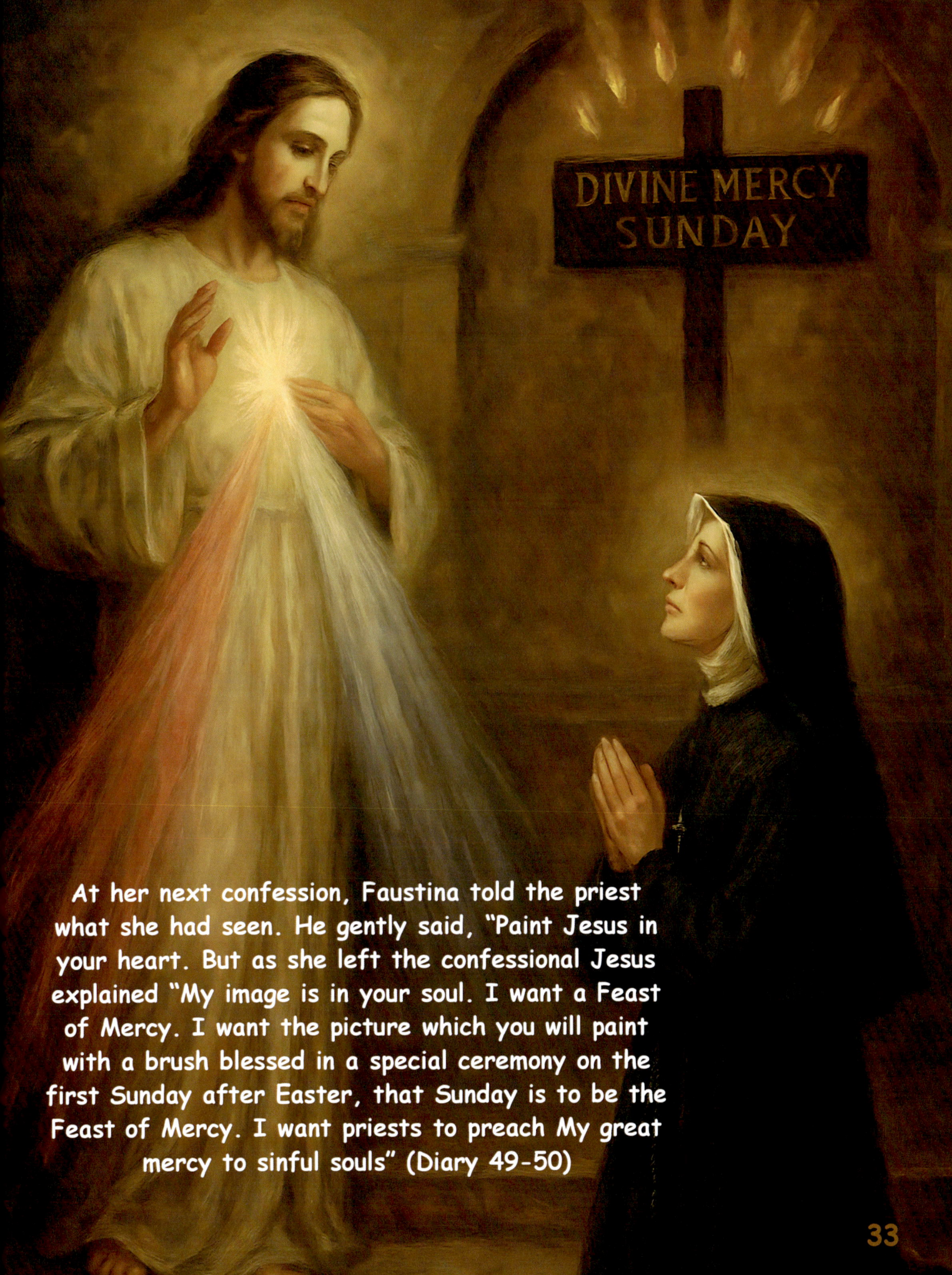

At her next confession, Faustina told the priest what she had seen. He gently said, "Paint Jesus in your heart. But as she left the confessional Jesus explained "My image is in your soul. I want a Feast of Mercy. I want the picture which you will paint with a brush blessed in a special ceremony on the first Sunday after Easter, that Sunday is to be the Feast of Mercy. I want priests to preach My great mercy to sinful souls" (Diary 49-50)

The lack of a permanent spiritual director and the inability to fulfill the tasks ascribed her made Sister Faustina want to back out of these supernatural inspirations, but Jesus patiently kept on explaining to her the magnitude of the work He had chosen her for. "Know that should you fail to have this picture painted and neglect all this work of mercy, on the Day of Judgement you shall be held to account for a great number of souls" (Diary 154)

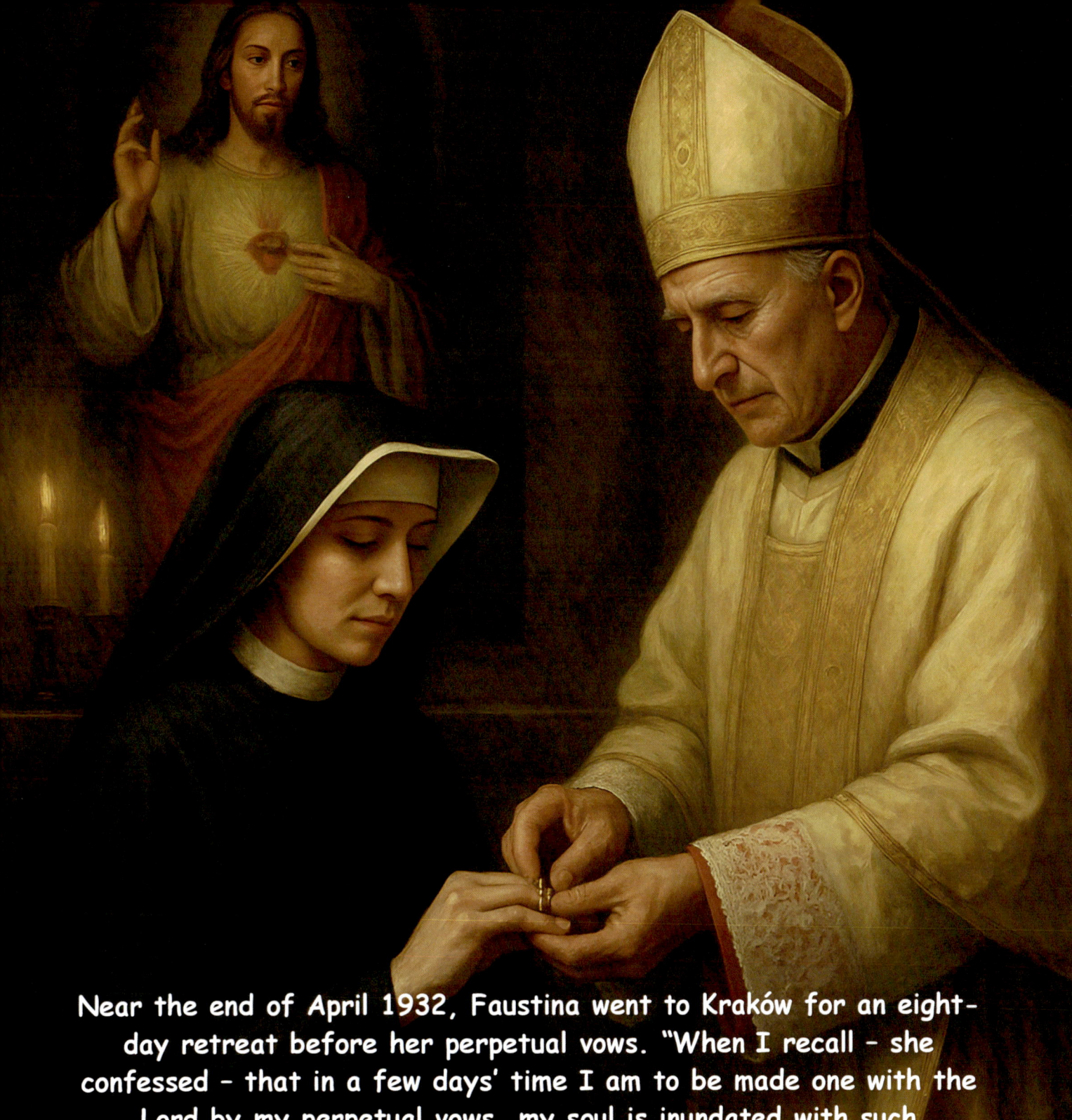

Near the end of April 1932, Faustina went to Kraków for an eight-day retreat before her perpetual vows. "When I recall – she confessed – that in a few days' time I am to be made one with the Lord by my perpetual vows, my soul is inundated with such unimaginable joy that I just can't describe it at all" (Diary 231) On May 1, 1933, Bishop Stanisław Rospond received her vows; she placed the Church, her community, family, sinners, the dying, and souls in purgatory into Jesus' Heart and asked Mary to be her mother in a special way. The bishop gave her a ring engraved "Jesus," showing she belonged to Christ forever—and from then on she felt even closer to His love

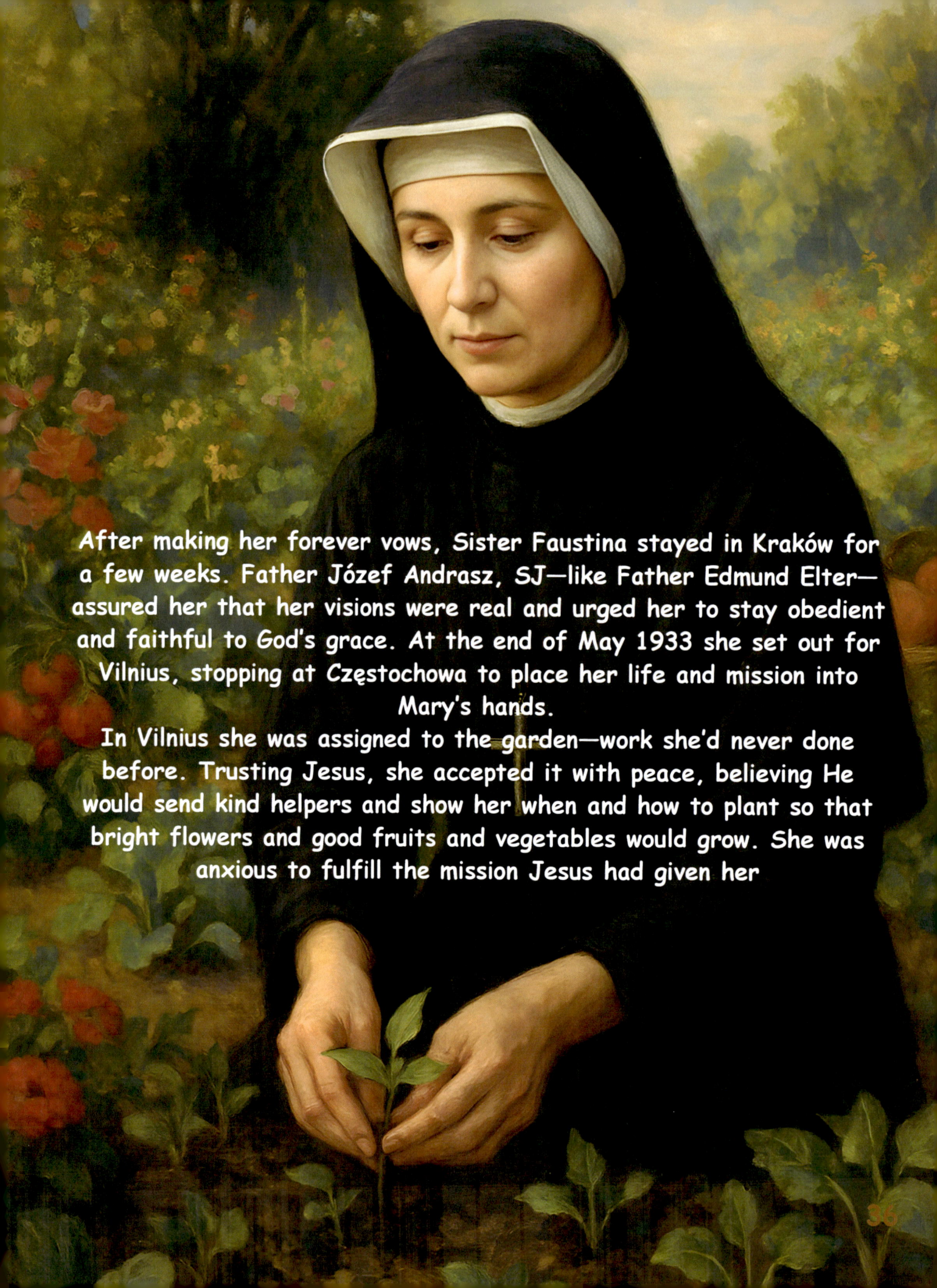

After making her forever vows, Sister Faustina stayed in Kraków for a few weeks. Father Józef Andrasz, SJ—like Father Edmund Elter—assured her that her visions were real and urged her to stay obedient and faithful to God's grace. At the end of May 1933 she set out for Vilnius, stopping at Częstochowa to place her life and mission into Mary's hands.

In Vilnius she was assigned to the garden—work she'd never done before. Trusting Jesus, she accepted it with peace, believing He would send kind helpers and show her when and how to plant so that bright flowers and good fruits and vegetables would grow. She was anxious to fulfill the mission Jesus had given her

Faustina waited for the priest Jesus had promised and the chance to have the painting of the Merciful Jesus made according to God's will. "The week for Confession came – she recorded in her diary – and, to my joy, I saw the priest whom I knew before I came to Vilnius. I had seen him in the vision. Then in my soul I heard these words, 'This is My faithful servant; he will help you carry out My will here on Earth'." (Diary 263). It was Father Michał Sopoćko, who lectured in pastoral theology in the Faculty of Theology of the Stefan Batory University, and in educational studies in a teachers' training college. He taught future priests at the university, served as a chaplain and spiritual director at the Vilnius seminary, and heard confessions for many religious communities—including Sister Faustina's house

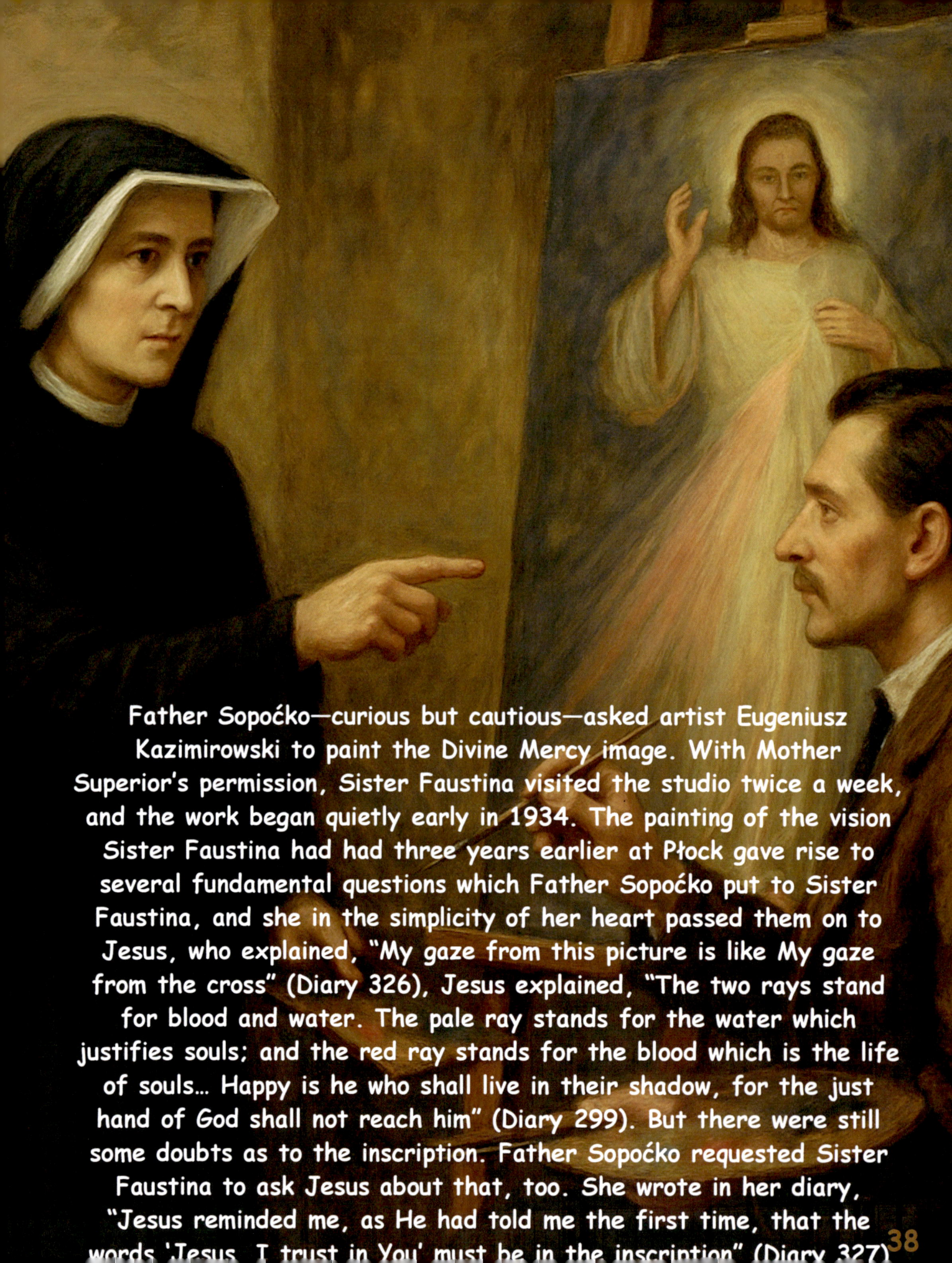

Father Sopoćko—curious but cautious—asked artist Eugeniusz Kazimirowski to paint the Divine Mercy image. With Mother Superior's permission, Sister Faustina visited the studio twice a week, and the work began quietly early in 1934. The painting of the vision Sister Faustina had had three years earlier at Płock gave rise to several fundamental questions which Father Sopoćko put to Sister Faustina, and she in the simplicity of her heart passed them on to Jesus, who explained, "My gaze from this picture is like My gaze from the cross" (Diary 326), Jesus explained, "The two rays stand for blood and water. The pale ray stands for the water which justifies souls; and the red ray stands for the blood which is the life of souls... Happy is he who shall live in their shadow, for the just hand of God shall not reach him" (Diary 299). But there were still some doubts as to the inscription. Father Sopoćko requested Sister Faustina to ask Jesus about that, too. She wrote in her diary, "Jesus reminded me, as He had told me the first time, that the words 'Jesus, I trust in You' must be in the inscription" (Diary 327)

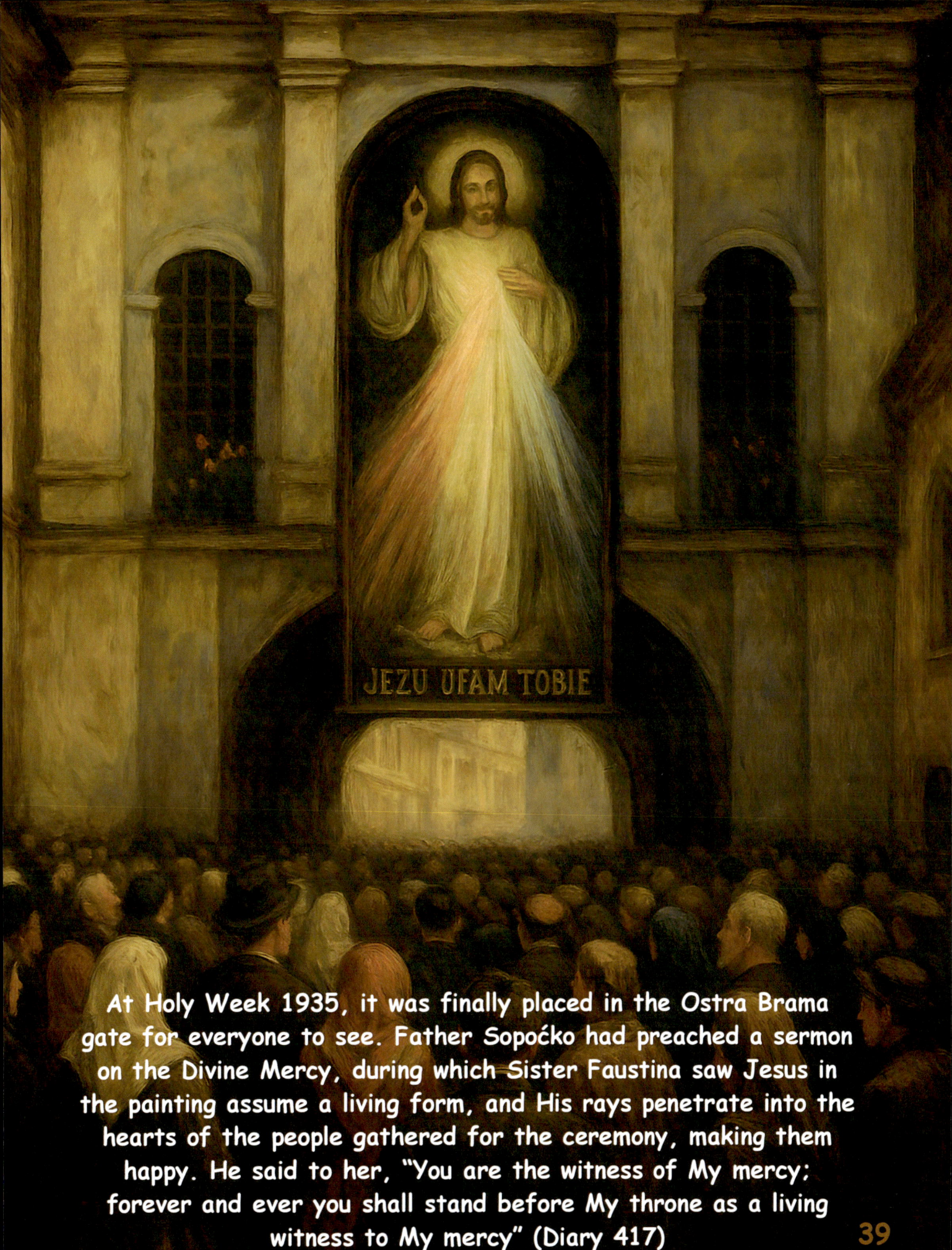

At Holy Week 1935, it was finally placed in the Ostra Brama gate for everyone to see. Father Sopoćko had preached a sermon on the Divine Mercy, during which Sister Faustina saw Jesus in the painting assume a living form, and His rays penetrate into the hearts of the people gathered for the ceremony, making them happy. He said to her, "You are the witness of My mercy; forever and ever you shall stand before My throne as a living witness to My mercy" (Diary 417)

39

On Friday, September 13, 1935, Sister Faustina saw an angel sent down by God to correct the world for its sins. Afraid for people, she begged God to show mercy. Jesus filled her heart with a special prayer—the words that became the Chaplet of Divine Mercy. As she prayed, the angel could no longer bring punishment, and Faustina understood how powerful God's mercy is for the whole world

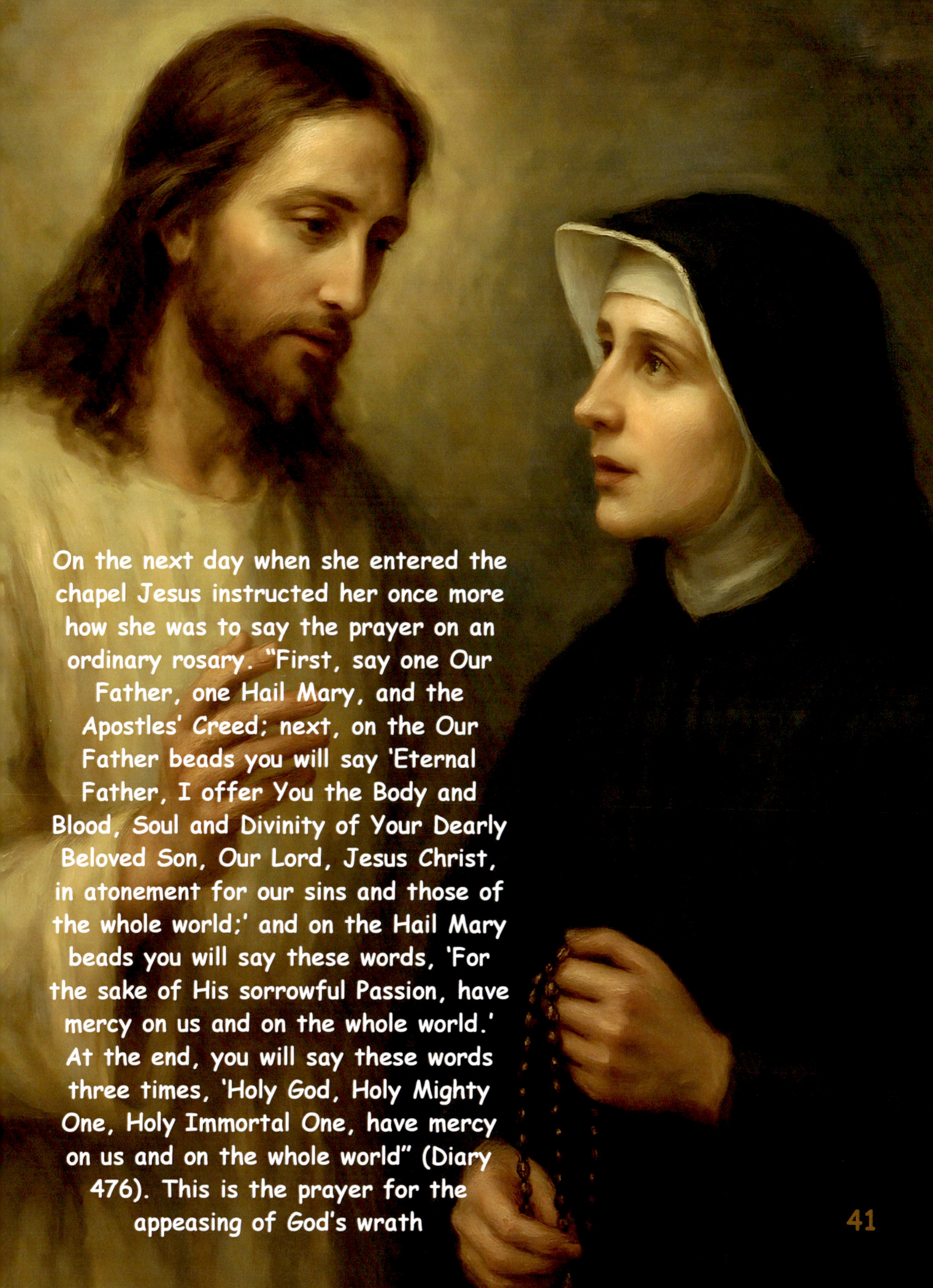

On the next day when she entered the chapel Jesus instructed her once more how she was to say the prayer on an ordinary rosary. "First, say one Our Father, one Hail Mary, and the Apostles' Creed; next, on the Our Father beads you will say 'Eternal Father, I offer You the Body and Blood, Soul and Divinity of Your Dearly Beloved Son, Our Lord, Jesus Christ, in atonement for our sins and those of the whole world;' and on the Hail Mary beads you will say these words, 'For the sake of His sorrowful Passion, have mercy on us and on the whole world.' At the end, you will say these words three times, 'Holy God, Holy Mighty One, Holy Immortal One, have mercy on us and on the whole world'" (Diary 476). This is the prayer for the appeasing of God's wrath

41

In the next visions Jesus made great promises to Sister Faustina in connection with the trustful reciting of the Chaplet. He promised the grace of a blessed and tranquil death not only to those who say the Chaplet, but also those at whose deathbed others will say the Chaplet. „Anyone who says the Chaplet just once, even should he be the most hardened of sinners, shall receive grace from My infinite mercy" (Diary 687). He said, "When they say this Chaplet, it will please Me to grant everything they shall ask for" (Diary 1541) 42

In the Vilnian period Jesus returned to the issue of the establishment of the Feast of Divine Mercy in the Church. He reminded Sister Faustina that He wanted it celebrated on the first Sunday after Easter, for souls were still being lost despite His bitter Passion. That day was to be the refuge for all souls, especially the poor sinners. "On that day the depths of My mercy are open; I pour out a whole sea of graces on souls that approach the fount of My mercy. Any soul that makes its Confession and receives Holy Communion will have its sins and its punishment completely remitted. On that day are open all the Divine floodgates through which graces flow; let no soul fear to approach Me, even if its sins be as scarlet" (Diary 699). Priests were to preach sermons on God's loving mercy for Man and make their hearts trust in Him, thereby enabling them to draw on the fountainhead of Divine Mercy. "Mankind shall not find peace and contentment until it turns with trust unto My mercy" (Diary 300), He told Sister Faustina

43

In the Cracovian convent Sister Faustina received the rest of the prophetic mission.In October 1937 Jesus gave Sister Faustina another form of worship of the Divine Mercy. He asked her to hold the moment of His death on the cross in veneration. "At three o'clock, beg for My mercy, especially for sinners, and immerse yourself, even for a short moment, in [contemplation on] My Passion, particularly when I was left forsaken at the moment of death. That is the hour of great mercy for the whole world" (Diary 1320)

His next apparition Jesus gave the details for this type of worship. He asked Sister Faustina to do the Stations of the Cross at the hour of His death, but if duty prevented this, to come to the chapel for a short moment of prayer before the Blessed Sacrament, and if even that was out of the question, to devote a brief moment to prayer wherever she was. With trustful prayer at three o'clock in the afternoon, offered on the merit of His Passion, is connected a promise of all graces which would be granted to the petitioners and all for whom they prayed, naturally provided that the grace asked for was in agreement with the will of God, i.e. that it is good for that person from the perspective of eternity. "Whatever you ask for at that hour, for yourself and for others, will be granted you; at that hour grace came upon the whole world – mercy superseded justice" (Diary 1572), He assured Sister Faustina

Jesus' request that she proclaim His Mercy to the world occurs time and again throughout the diary."Tell the world of My mercy, of My love. The flames of mercy are burning Me; I want to pour them out onto human souls. Oh, what pain they cause Me when they do not want to accept My mercy. Do what is in your power to spread the worship of My mercy; I shall complete whatever is wanting in your capacity. Tell distressed humankind to come up and cling to My Heart, and I shall fill it with peace. Tell them, O My daughter, that I am love and mercy itself" (Diary 1074). Jesus said, "I protect souls that spread the worship of My Mercy throughout their lives, as a loving mother protects her baby; and at the hour of their death I shall not be a Judge unto them, but their merciful Saviour" (Diary 1075)

As Jesus told her, His request that God's merciful love for mankind be preached is the last recourse for many souls, which are being lost notwithstanding His bitter Passion. It is also the means to establish peace in human hearts and between nations: "Mankind shall not find peace and contentment until it turns with trust unto My mercy" (Diary 300). And it is to prepare the world for His second coming. "No-one can deny that God is infinitely merciful; He wants everyone to know that. Before He comes again as Judge, He wants souls to learn that He is the King of mercy" (Diary 378), Sister Faustina wrote in her diary

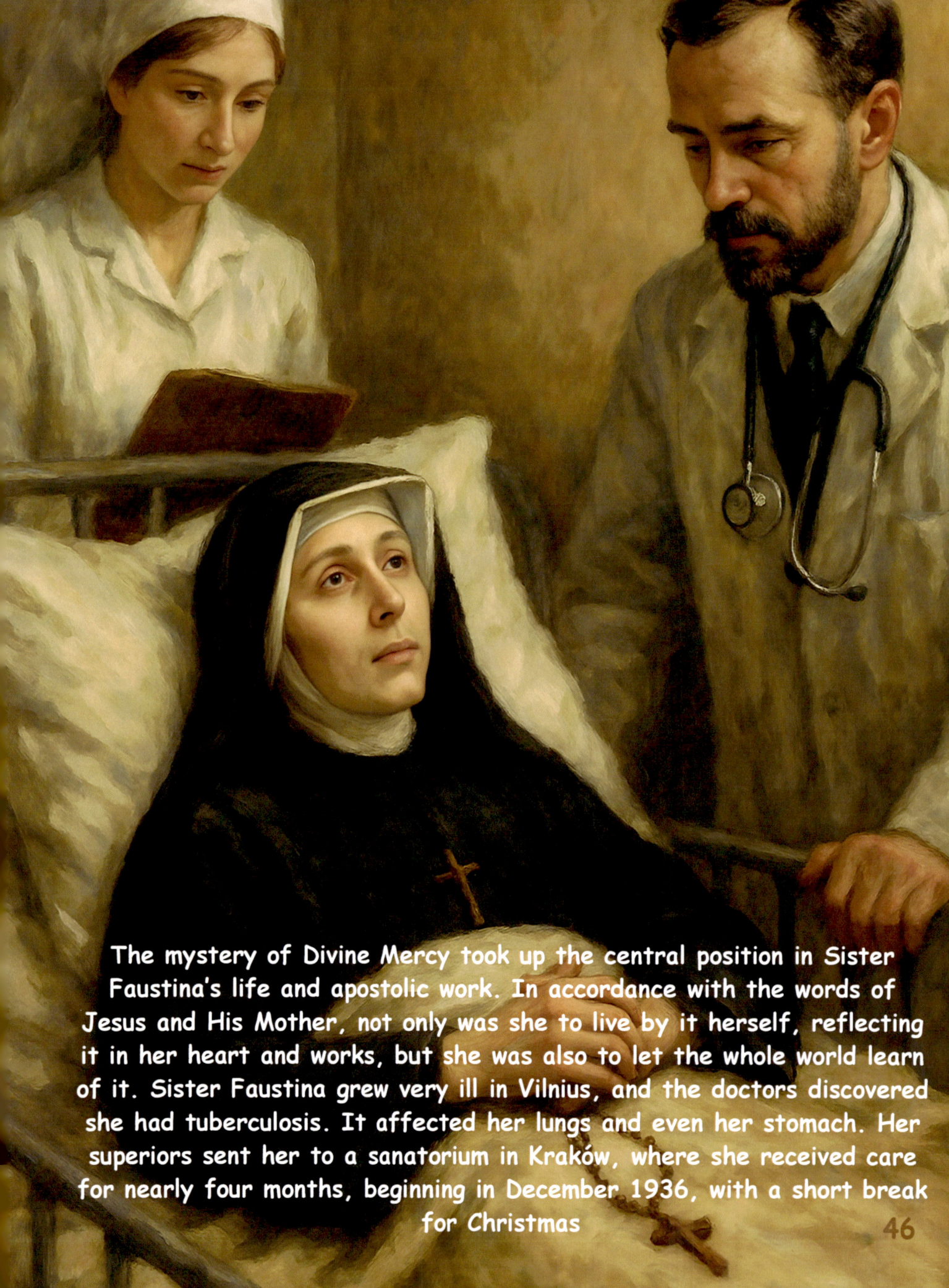

The mystery of Divine Mercy took up the central position in Sister Faustina's life and apostolic work. In accordance with the words of Jesus and His Mother, not only was she to live by it herself, reflecting it in her heart and works, but she was also to let the whole world learn of it. Sister Faustina grew very ill in Vilnius, and the doctors discovered she had tuberculosis. It affected her lungs and even her stomach. Her superiors sent her to a sanatorium in Kraków, where she received care for nearly four months, beginning in December 1936, with a short break for Christmas

46

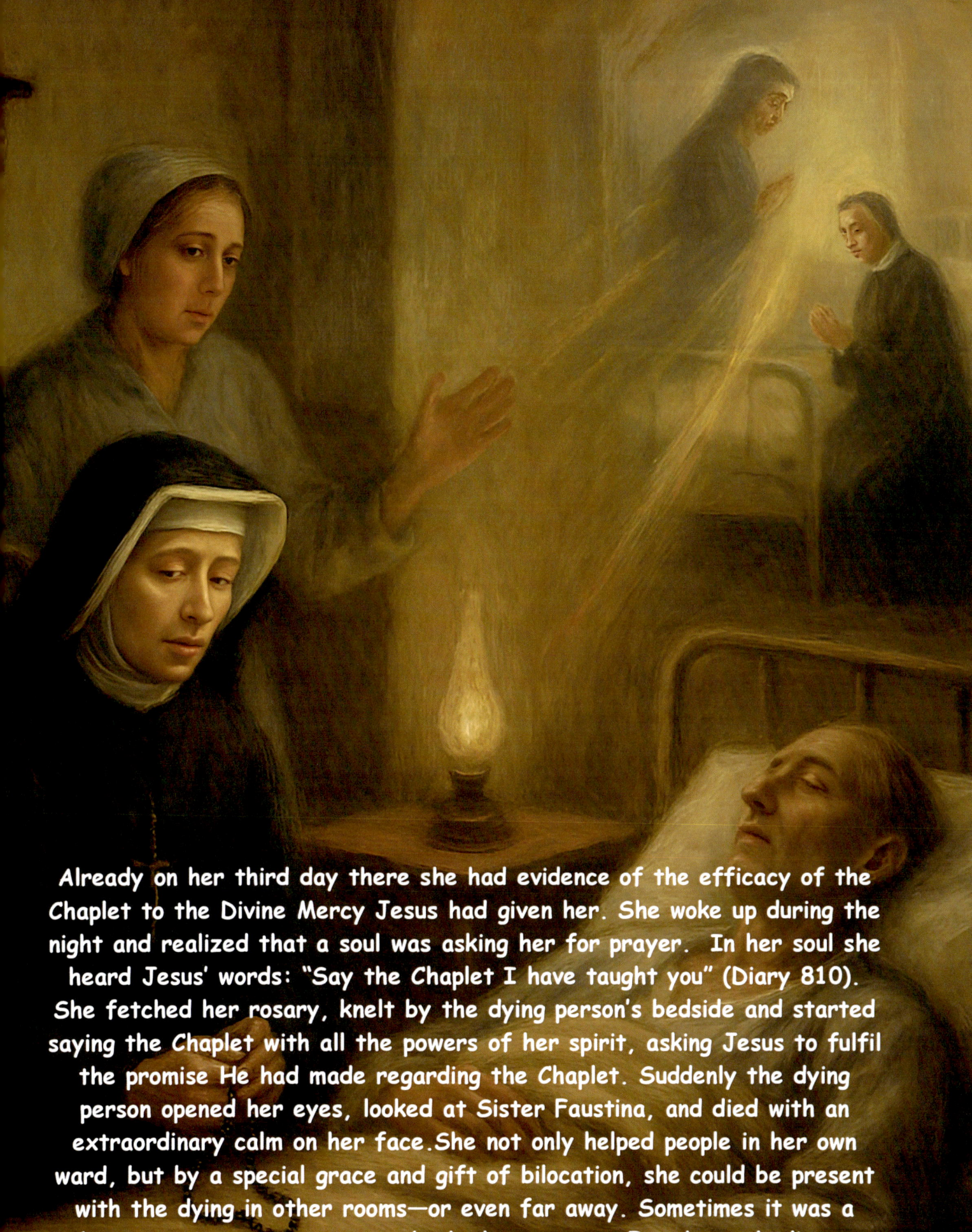

Already on her third day there she had evidence of the efficacy of the Chaplet to the Divine Mercy Jesus had given her. She woke up during the night and realized that a soul was asking her for prayer. In her soul she heard Jesus' words: "Say the Chaplet I have taught you" (Diary 810). She fetched her rosary, knelt by the dying person's bedside and started saying the Chaplet with all the powers of her spirit, asking Jesus to fulfil the promise He had made regarding the Chaplet. Suddenly the dying person opened her eyes, looked at Sister Faustina, and died with an extraordinary calm on her face. She not only helped people in her own ward, but by a special grace and gift of bilocation, she could be present with the dying in other rooms—or even far away. Sometimes it was a relative, a sister, or someone she had never met. For the soul, distance doesn't stand in the way

Even while she suffered in body and soul, God gave Sister Faustina many hidden graces. Now and then, someone else caught a glimpse. Sister Kajetana once visited her at Prądnik. She knocked but heard no reply, so she gently opened the door. There, to her amazement, she saw Faustina changed—raised above the bed, looking far off as if at something unseen. Frightened, Sister Kajetana stood by the small bedside altar until, a moment later, Faustina returned to herself and smiled, "Oh, Sister, you've come—please come in

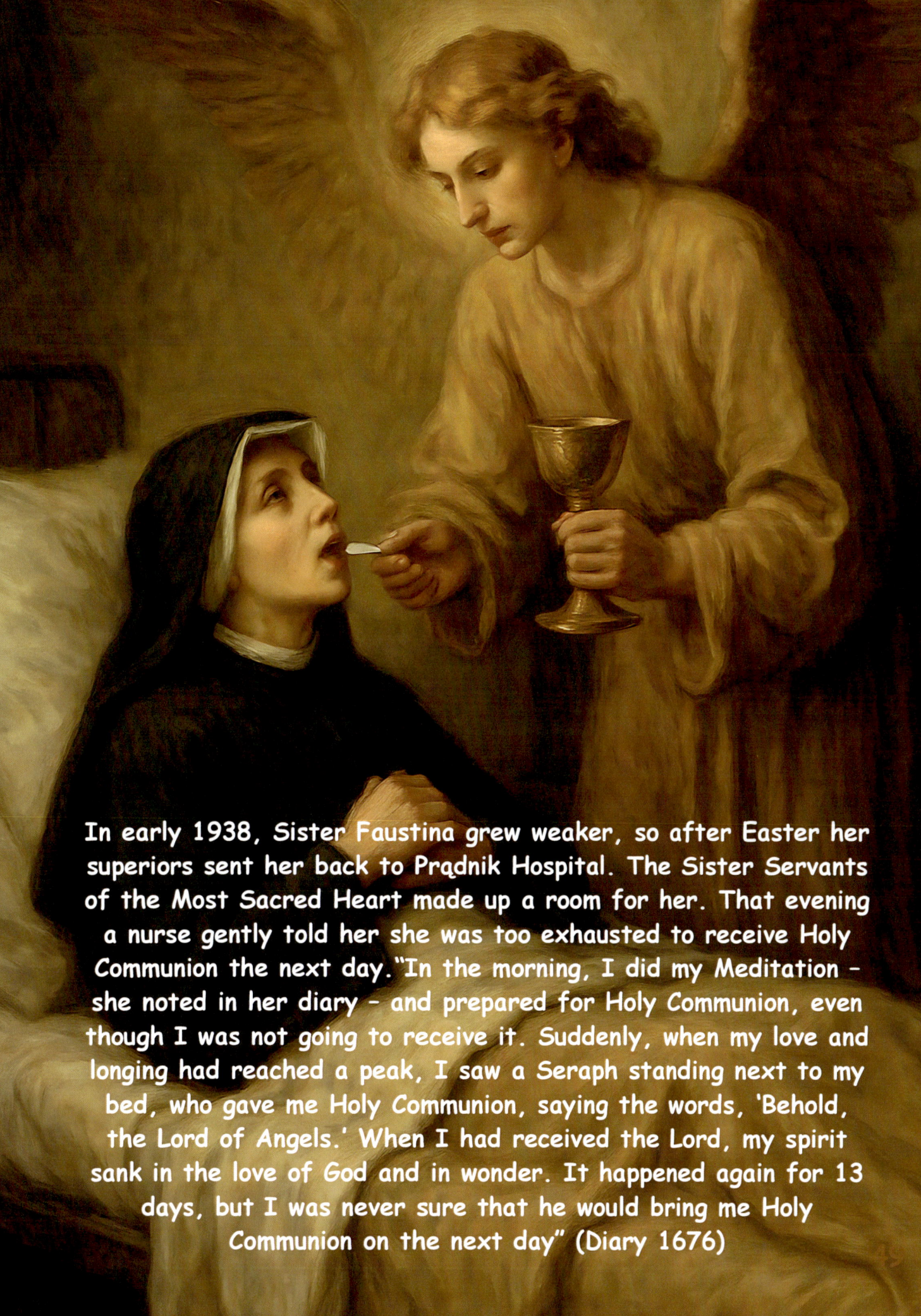

In early 1938, Sister Faustina grew weaker, so after Easter her superiors sent her back to Prądnik Hospital. The Sister Servants of the Most Sacred Heart made up a room for her. That evening a nurse gently told her she was too exhausted to receive Holy Communion the next day."In the morning, I did my Meditation – she noted in her diary – and prepared for Holy Communion, even though I was not going to receive it. Suddenly, when my love and longing had reached a peak, I saw a Seraph standing next to my bed, who gave me Holy Communion, saying the words, 'Behold, the Lord of Angels.' When I had received the Lord, my spirit sank in the love of God and in wonder. It happened again for 13 days, but I was never sure that he would bring me Holy Communion on the next day" (Diary 1676)

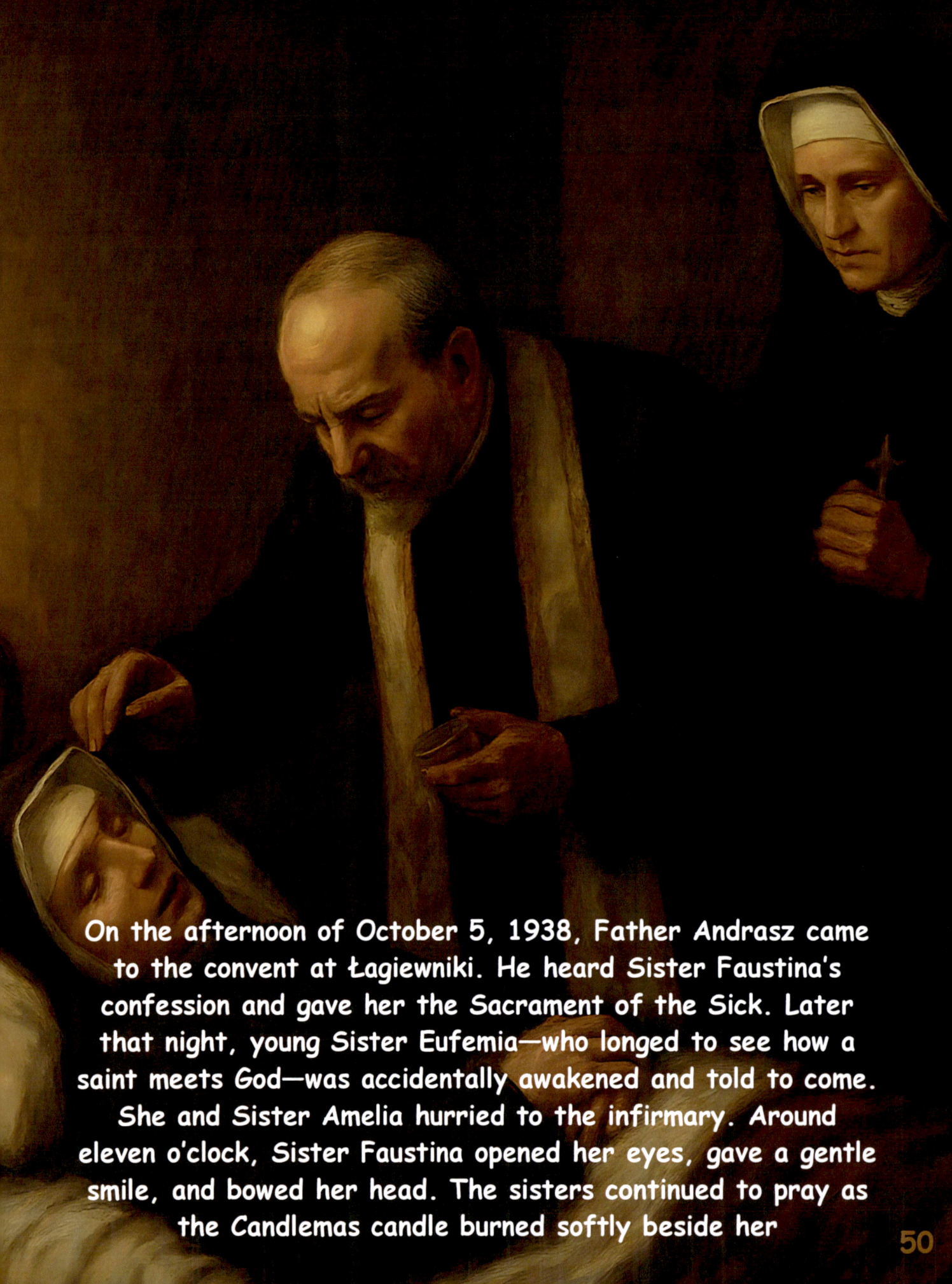

On the afternoon of October 5, 1938, Father Andrasz came to the convent at Łagiewniki. He heard Sister Faustina's confession and gave her the Sacrament of the Sick. Later that night, young Sister Eufemia—who longed to see how a saint meets God—was accidentally awakened and told to come. She and Sister Amelia hurried to the infirmary. Around eleven o'clock, Sister Faustina opened her eyes, gave a gentle smile, and bowed her head. The sisters continued to pray as the Candlemas candle burned softly beside her

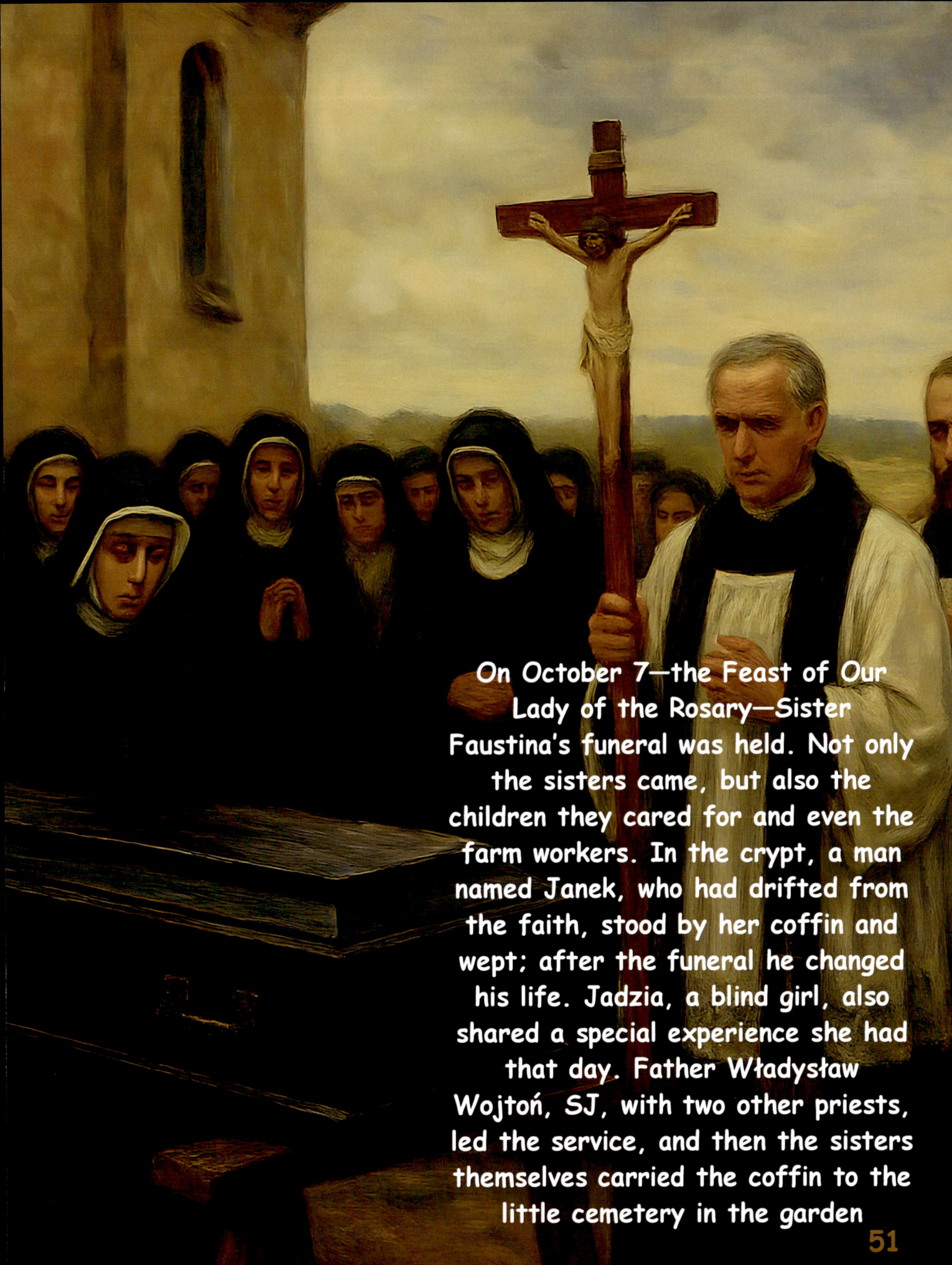

On October 7—the Feast of Our Lady of the Rosary—Sister Faustina's funeral was held. Not only the sisters came, but also the children they cared for and even the farm workers. In the crypt, a man named Janek, who had drifted from the faith, stood by her coffin and wept; after the funeral he changed his life. Jadzia, a blind girl, also shared a special experience she had that day. Father Władysław Wojtoń, SJ, with two other priests, led the service, and then the sisters themselves carried the coffin to the little cemetery in the garden

51

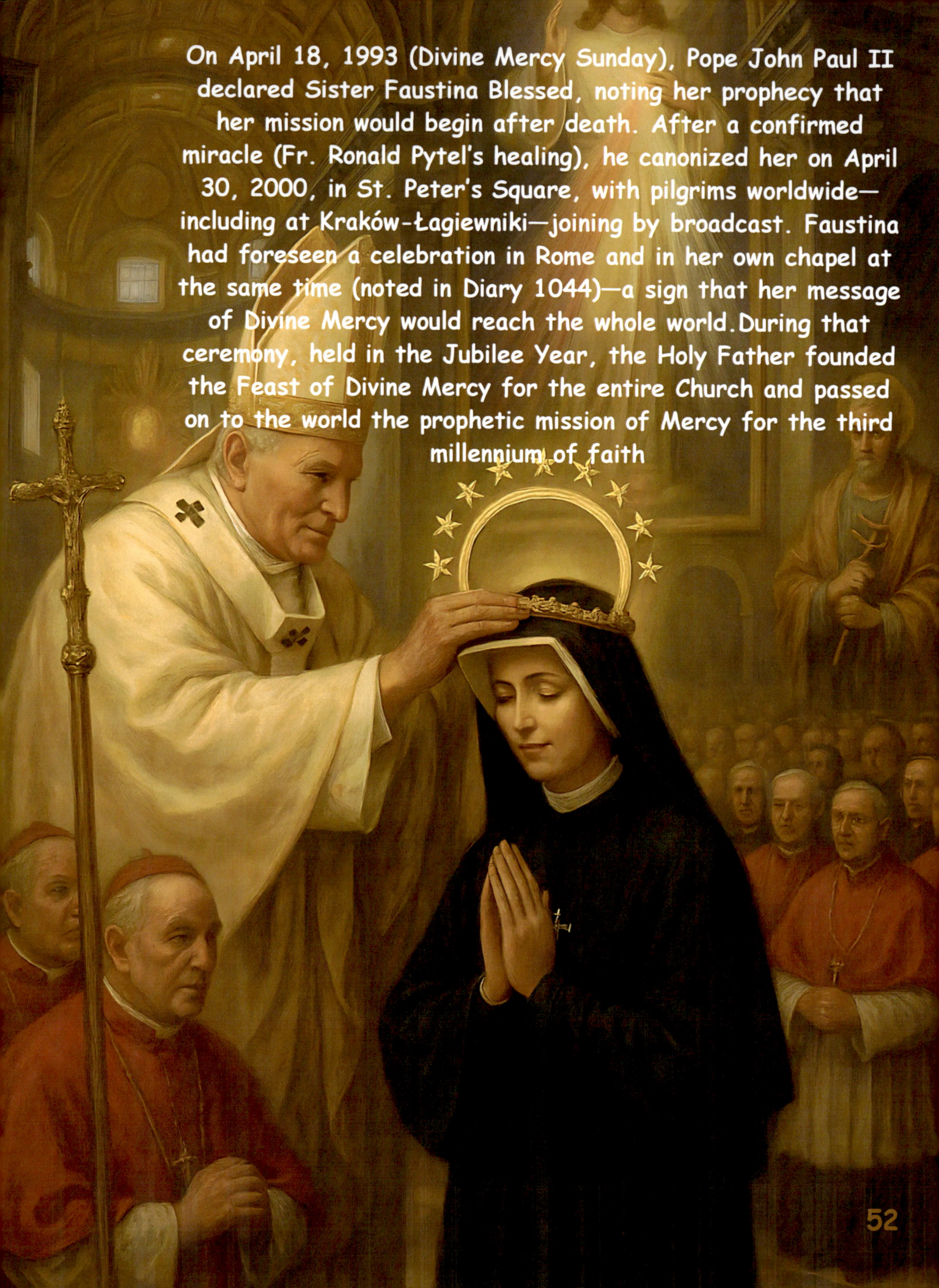

On April 18, 1993 (Divine Mercy Sunday), Pope John Paul II declared Sister Faustina Blessed, noting her prophecy that her mission would begin after death. After a confirmed miracle (Fr. Ronald Pytel's healing), he canonized her on April 30, 2000, in St. Peter's Square, with pilgrims worldwide—including at Kraków-Łagiewniki—joining by broadcast. Faustina had foreseen a celebration in Rome and in her own chapel at the same time (noted in Diary 1044)—a sign that her message of Divine Mercy would reach the whole world. During that ceremony, held in the Jubilee Year, the Holy Father founded the Feast of Divine Mercy for the entire Church and passed on to the world the prophetic mission of Mercy for the third millennium of faith

HOW TO RECITE THE DIVINE MERCY CHAPLET FOR KIDS

1. Make the Sign of the Cross
In the name of the Father, and of the Son, and of the Holy Spirit. Amen.

2. Opening Prayer (Optional for Kids)
Jesus, I trust in You, Please have mercy on us and the whole world.

3. On the First Large Bead
Say the "Our Father"
Say the "Hail Mary."

Hail Mary, full of grace,
the Lord is with thee;
blessed art thou among women,
and blessed is the fruit of thy
womb, Jesus.

4. On the Next Large Bead

Say the "Apostles' Creed
In simple form.

5. On Each Large Bead Before a Decade
Say once: "Eternal Father. I offer You the Body and **blood** Soul and Divinity of Your dearly beloved Son, our Lord Jesus Christ, in atonement for our sins and those of the whole world.

7. On Each of the 10 Small Beads
Say ten times:"For the sake of His sorrowful Passion, have mercy on us and on the whole world.

8. Repeat All 5 Decades
(1 "Eternal Father" + 10 "For the sake..." = one decaade)

Help Helena find her way back to the chapel through a garden maze

ST. FAUSTINA WORD SEARCH

```
A Q H C Z X T S V X
F A U S T I N A N V
M E R C Y F A U S T
D I A R Y J E S U S
D I A R Y J E S U S
F A U S T I N A R C
E S U S P A D L O
P A D L O C K
```

MERCY

TRUST

FAUSTINA

DIARY

Guide the seraph carrying the Eucharist through the hospital ward to Faustina's bed

JESUS, I TRUST IN YOU

61

MY MERCY PLEDGE

Today I will show mercy by

❶ Where was Saint Faustina born?
Ⓐ Warsaw   Ⓑ GŁOGOWIEC   Ⓒ Kraków

_____

❷ Faustina's special message from Jesus is called the
"Divine _____."
Ⓐ Promise   Ⓑ Mercy   Ⓒ Power

_____

❸ T / F   Saint Faustina sometimes woke up at night
to kneel and pray.

_____

❹ At which hour did Jesus ask Faustina to pray in a
special way?
Ⓐ 9 a.m.   Ⓑ 3 p.m.   Ⓒ Midnight

_____

❺ Which prayer did Jesus teach Faustina using ordinary
rosary beads?
Ⓐ The Rosary   Ⓑ The Chaplet of Divine Mercy   Ⓒ The Angelus

_____

❻ T / F   After her First Holy Communion Faustina said,
"I'm not alone— I'm walking with Jesus."

_____

★ M Y   S C O R E ★
_____ / 6 correct

◇ A N S W E R   K E Y ◇
1 − B 2 − B 3 − T
4 − B 5 − B 6 − T

⋄ D I V I N E M E R C Y Q U I Z ⋄
(Circle the answer or mark T / F, then color!)

❶ Which prayer begins the Divine Mercy Chaplet?
   Ⓐ Our Father   Ⓑ Hail Holy Queen   Ⓒ Memorare

_____

❷ On each small (Hail—Mary) bead we pray:
   "For the sake of His _____ Passion,
    have mercy on us and on the whole world."
   Ⓐ Joyful   Ⓑ Sorrowful   Ⓒ Glorious

_____

❸ T / F You can pray the Chaplet on a regular five-decade rosary.

_____

❹ What three words appear beneath the Divine Mercy image?
   Ⓐ "God Is Love"   Ⓑ "Jesus, I Trust in You"   Ⓒ "Peace Be Still"

_____

❺ Which hour did Jesus call the "Hour of Mercy"?
   Ⓐ Noon   Ⓑ 3:00 p.m.   Ⓒ Sunset

_____

❻ T / F Jesus promised mercy "in life and at the hour of death"
   to those who pray the Chaplet with trust.

_____

★ M Y S C O R E ★

_____ / 6

⋄ A N S W E R S ⋄
1—A 2—B 3—T
4—B 5—B 6—T

CERTIFICATE
OF COMPLETION

Name _____

Date _____   Signature

_____

Saint Faustina Activity Book

Dr. Diya Abraham, Ph.D

A researcher at heart and mentor by calling, Dr. Diya Abraham earned her doctorate in Neuroscience from the Max Planck Institute in Germany and completed a post-doctoral fellowship at the University of California, San Francisco. Her work on circadian rhythms—the genes that keep our inner clocks in sync—has appeared in leading peer-reviewed journals and has been showcased on international conference stages

Dr. Abraham weaves science into faith-infused learning experiences. Through Bee Little Curious, the company she founded to enrich curious minds & soul, she creates evidence-based educational resources and uplifting religious products. She partners with parish schools to embed STEM principles into grace-filled curricula

Joby James

Joby James has built an illustrious career at the intersection of engineering, enterprise-class cybersecurity sales and tech entrepreneurship. As the founder of cybersecurity firm, his team helps companies safeguard data while equipping organizations to navigate the digital world safely and responsibly

Joby believes that safeguarding souls matters just as much as protecting systems—a conviction nurtured through years of mentoring youth groups, where he first shared the saint stories that now inspire his writing

Enquiries: info@beelittlecurious.com

9 781969 238024